MW00679361

With love and gratitude to Susie Hickman and Debbie Miller, good teachers and friends, who reawakened my passion for teaching and learning.

—*CCO*

In loving memory of my father, Charles A. Reilly, mentor, teacher, and school principal.

—*ERM*

AUTHORS' NOTE

Where a reference to gender was unavoidable, we elected to use the feminine because of the current and historic prevalence of female teachers. We intend no slight to male teachers; moreover, we applaud their growing ranks. We look forward to a day when the teaching profession is free of gender stereotypes and our children will benefit from good female *and* male mentors in all grades.

For _____

From _____

You are a good teacher because. . .

A good teacher opens my eyes to this whole planet.

LIGHT SUN

A good teacher waits for us in the classroom
before school starts.

A good teacher knows everybody has a bad day now and then.

A good teacher knows when *I'm* having a bad day.

A good teacher likes me to share what I know.

A good teacher is patient when
I can't remember which way the "b" goes.

A good teacher helps us understand that
we all learn differently.

A good teacher knows how I learn best.

Terrific work!

A good teacher tells me when I do a good job

Fantastic!

and

Nice job!

You did it!

Super

WOW

celebrates with me when I learn something new.

A good teacher makes me glad to be me.

A good teacher's voice
keeps telling me,

"Do your best.
Do your very best."

Dear Children:

This is the first of many pages we have saved for you

to write and draw something special for your teacher.

Whenever you see apples marching in this book, it is

your time to be the writer and illustrator. Have fun!

Love Oliver
Ellen McCormick

A good teacher is quiet in the library, too.

A good teacher helps us learn
to treat each other with respect.

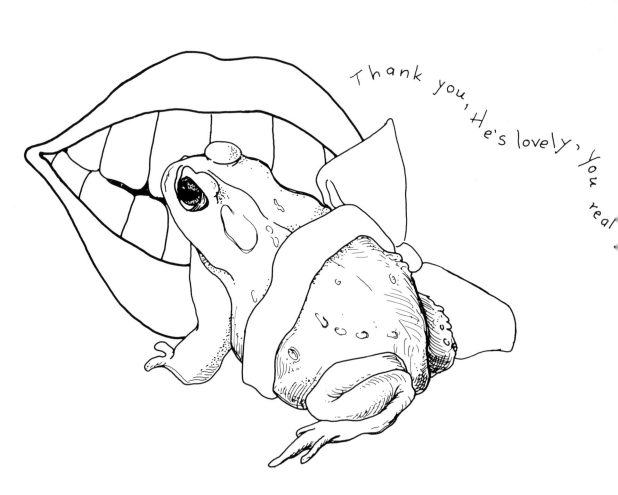

Thank you, He's lovely, You real

houldn't have

A good teacher loves my presents.

A good teacher reminds me
to water my science project
before it's too late.

A good teacher lets me try

Gone with the Wind

because my grandmother

said she liked it.

A good teacher gives us all good hugs.

A good teacher is never *too* tired or *too* busy.

A good teacher remembers
I am left-handed.

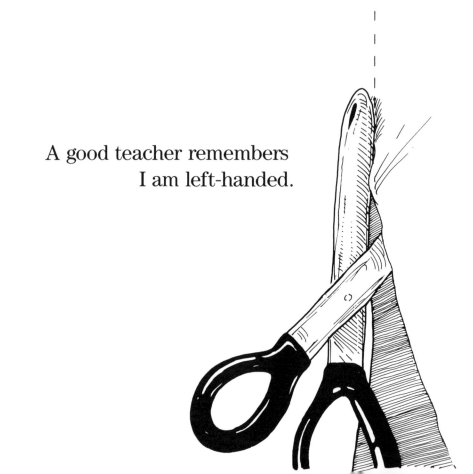

A good teacher knows what
we'll be doing next Thursday.

A good teacher has me find my own mistakes.

Super

Being Nice to Others

Clay 4/2/91

Being nice to others is not (comenting) alot it just is treating them like one of your best friends even when they aren't. A best friend is someone you care about alot and hope the best for them. If you treat them nice and they don't the (qeschin) is why do you give your (repect) to them.

A good teacher tells us

when she's proud of us.

A good teacher gives me

an awesome choice of vegetables

when I won't be a mushroom

in the school play.

A good teacher wants to know what *I* think.

A good teacher mixes math and reading

and spelling

and music

and science

together.

A good teacher *writes with us*.

A good teacher laughs when things are funny

and doesn't laugh when thin

aren't funny.

A good teacher looks into my eyes when we're talking.

A good teacher smiles and winks when I'm on stage and feeling very nervous.

A good teacher makes comfortable places for us to read.

A good teacher can find my other mitten—

sometimes.

A good teacher gives me t i m e to answer her questions.

A good teacher listens to all sides. A good teacher listens to all sides. A good teacher listens to all sides. A good teacher listens to all sides. A good teacher listens. A good teacher listens to all sides. A good teacher listens to all sides. A good teacher listens to all sides.

A good teacher asks me HOW

so I can figure out WHY.

• one bottle of glue • tape dispenser • scissors • an apple for the teacher • photograph of the class • papers to be read • blue pencil • ladybug specimens • letter from our British pen pal • magnifying glass • pencil holder • pens and pencils • coffee mug • star and heart stickers • erasers • bird feather • comb and brush • confiscated cherry bomb • confiscated firecracker • spare nickels for milk money • softball signed by the class • a yo-yo • wasp nest • tissues • tacks • keys • pushpins • bird nest • empty robin eggs • safety pins • paper clips • clothespins • spare pair of shoes • first aid kit • extra clothes for mud puddle days • hat • tote bags • files for field trips, guests, pen pals, and projects • craft paper • gloves • calendar • soda cans • needle and thread • envelopes • marbles • adhesive strips

A good teacher makes things that happened a long time ago interesting and not boring.

A good teacher teaches us to teach each other.

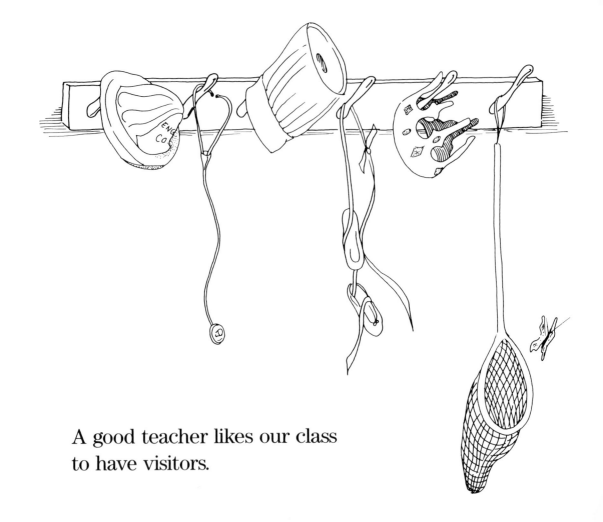

A good teacher likes our class
to have visitors.

A good teacher learns from us.

A good teacher SHOWS us.

A good teacher thinks s$^{n\,a}$k$_{e\,s}$ and rats make terrific pets.

A good teacher gets me thinking in other

directions.

A good teacher acts the same around the principal,
the custodian,
the school nurse,
and other teachers.

A good teacher is nice to all the kids in school.

A good teacher celebrates all our holidays.

A good teacher is glad to see my parents —and my parents know it.

A good teacher laughs at my knock-knock jokes.

A good teacher makes us feel like...

A good teacher helps us understand
that everybody's best is not the same.

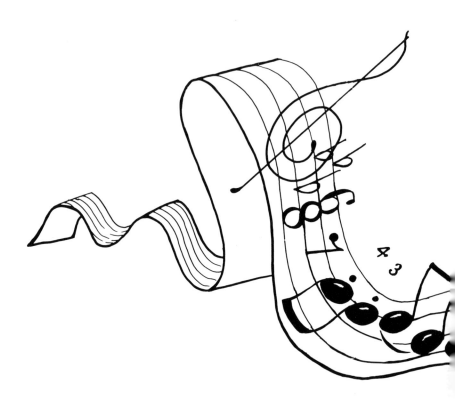

A good teacher makes Beethoven come *alive!*

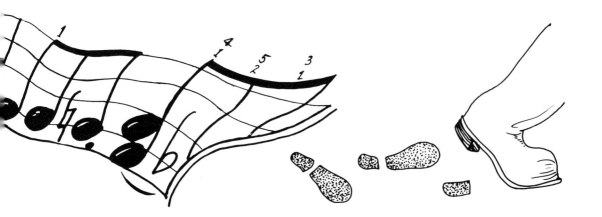

A good teacher makes sure

I know what's going on.

A good teacher goes to school, too.

A good teacher wants us *all* to have fun in gym class.

A good teacher knows all families are real families.

A good teacher helps us talk about stuff that worries us.

A good teacher gets dirty on field trips.

A good teacher is still my friend
after I let the ladybugs out for recess.

A good teacher helps me hunt for my retainer.

A good teacher wants us all to have our dreams.

A good teacher knows when I'm embarrassed.

It's *good* to have a good teacher!!!

Dear _____

You are my good teacher because. . .

_____

_____

_____

_____

AFTERWORD

This book had its inception in the spring of 1990. I wanted to understand how teachers like my son's excellent second grade teacher, Susie Hickman, managed to generate and sustain excitement for learning. To that end, I interviewed her students, many of their parents, and a number of Mrs. Hickman's colleagues to discover their perceptions of good teaching. I especially wish to thank the following children from that second grade class—and their parents—for sharing their thoughts on good teachers: Sean, Cy, Lauren, Mark, Grahame, Lizzie, Sarah, Timmy, Jacob, Ann Sydney, Melissa, Bo, Elizabeth, Clay, Scott, Sally, Alden, Alison, Mary Gordon, and Marty. Let there be no doubt that even young children know what good teaching is about and appreciate it.

I have been privileged also to observe closely and learn from the work of another excellent teacher, Debbie Miller, during my son's third grade year. It is fitting that Clay's experiences and my observations of the past two years—as educator and parent—have found their way to the pages of *A Good Teacher*.

—*CCO*